The Ecstasy of Regret

The Ecstasy of Regret

Poems by
Dannye Romine Powell

THE UNIVERSITY OF ARKANSAS PRESS

FAYETTEVILLE   2002

06   05   04   03   02   5   4   3   2   1

Designed by Ellen Beeler

☺ The paper used in this publication meets the minimum requirements of
the American National Standard for Permanence of Paper for Printed
Library Materials Z39.48-1984.

Library of Congress Cataloging-in-Publication Data

Powell, Dannye Romine.
    The ecstasy of regret : poems / by Dannye Romine Powell.
      p. cm.
    ISBN 1–55728–734–1 (pbk. : alk. paper)
    I. Title.
    PS3566.O8267 E28 2002
    811'.54—dc21

                                                          2002007150

For Patrick

Acknowledgments

Grateful acknowledgment is made to the editors of the following publications, in which these poems first appeared, some in slightly different versions: *Field:* "A Reason to Embrace Sorrow" and "Wake the Tree"; *Folio:* "Long Distance"; *Green Mountains Review:* "Better to Know the Woodcutter Might Never Arrive at the Cottage"; *Kalliope:* "How the Muse Keeps Trying to Elude Me"; *New Republic:* "The Other Life"; *Ploughshares:* "The Woman Who Allowed Light to Have Its Way with Her"; *Poetry:* "She Never Thought of Vegetables" and "Deprivation"; *Prairie Schooner:* "At a Flea Market, A Woman Buys a Letter Postmarked 1944, From Sybil Reed to Louis Mack", "Relapse", and "The Reconstructed Breast"; *River Styx:* "I Hang Up the Phone after Hearing I Have Cancer"; *Sow's Ear:* "Dread Begs to Fondle Your Breasts"; *Tar River Poetry Review:* "The Chair Where I Sat Reading While My Parents Made Love."

"The Other Life" appeared in *No Hiding Place: Uncovering the Legacy of Charlotte Writers: An Anthology.* Edited by Frye Gaillard, Amy Rogers, and Robert Inman. Down Home Press, 1999.

Grateful acknowledgment is also made to the National Endowment for the Arts and to the North Carolina Arts Council for poetry fellowships, which made the writing of these poems possible.

My great thanks to Enid Shomer for her gifted and inspiring editing, and to Susan Ludvigson, Judy Goldman, Julie Suk, Lucinda Grey, Mary Hunter Daly, Dede Wilson, Sharon Reardon, and Gaye Ingram for their invaluable criticism of the poems.

Contents

A Seamless Forgetting

Suffused in the Heat

The Vaster Blue

A Seamless Forgetting

What Entices May Finally Recede

I took a picture of a farm house
the way you do on vacation. Nothing
adventurous. It didn't capture
the dusky mountain
that swarmed up the sky, dwarfing
the meadow and lending perspective
to dawn, even desire. It did catch
the gravel path and the road
no longer there, smoothed over
now with grass. Just a house,
I tell you. A house where I longed
to rattle dishes and remake
the bed. I say I took one picture.
I took two. The one where
I stood farther back
shows the longer road, its slow curve,
how the house appears to dream
against the shawl of a blue-green forest.
What you miss in this distant view—
what you might never see—the bevel
of wear on the wooden steps,
the two white chairs on the porch,
the iron lock that makes a traitor of the door.

Startled by Green

I pull the mango low
so my father's camera
can better catch
its muscled ripeness,
its sunrise skin.
My son, who is five,
slips in beside me. He wears
a striped shirt and aims high
his model airplane.

After my father dies,
I find that photo in his desk,
and by December light
it seems new and bold—
June's uncanny green,
sun climbing the neighbor's wall,
the boy's grin a tease,
insisting he'll never go wrong,
and all that fruit suspended midair.

The Absence of Lake

The lake entered,
its silver numbing me

as I dreamed. So silent
and swift an overtaking

not even the shore noticed.
I breathed. The lake

breathed. A seamless forgetting.
Somewhere in the night

it drained, level by jagged level,
revealing first the tops

of scrub oak, the gnarl
and stump of ancient wood,

the lawn chair blown off the pier
last summer, its stretched

and ragged webbing,
the lampshade the neighbor rubbed

with lemon juice and left
beneath the pines to bleach,

mud-streaked now and damp,
fastened in needles of light.

Eve Screams for the Hoe

Yes he is lean
lean and dark
but his meat
is not so lean
clean up in her
she can feel him
not so lean
while Adam tries
and tries
to find the hoe
she screamed for
when the serpent
first came calling
dark and lean
before he came
clean up in her
while Adam tried
and tried
to find the hoe

The Woman Who Allowed Light to Have Its Way with Her

She remembers
an absence of blue
billowing down,
playing loose with her,
the impetuous sailor
her mother warned her against
time after time. The light
did not invite her to dance,
nor shine upon her only.
In countless borrowed rooms
she swallowed its gleaming
intimations. Later, in the dark,
she lies on the bed,
recalling the silvery edge
of its breath, like birch trees
in spring. She sparkles with shame.

The Day He Disappeared

I was eating gazpacho
from a glass bowl. So unlike me
to fix myself a tray,
heat the bread, fold
an aqua napkin. Each spoonful
was a walled garden, a fountain
in Spain. As I reached
to answer the phone,
I was absently dreaming
of more such bounty
in the weeks ahead. I listened,
barely spoke. Out my window,
pin oaks conspired
in a shady stain, traffic
slowed. I did not know
and did not want to know
how a summer's day can twist
in the drift of a leaf
and spread my bread with cold.

How the Muse Keeps Trying to Elude Me

Why we chose Richmond
I'll never know, but there we were

in a hotel, making love all weekend,
you kissing me even while I dozed.

By Sunday, you were losing interest.
I love you, I said, hoping to win you back.

Nothing. *Will we see each other again?*
I asked, my petulance showing

like a cotton slip. We bantered about time.
You said we had only an hour

to catch the plane. I knew we had more,
and our argument grew tedious.

Less than a year later
you were sneaking

in the back door of that motel
by the lake then not showing up

as promised and me just as optimistic

when you came back again,

this time to my parents'

living room where I begged you

to put away your racing form

and sway with me in the ripe spill

of music, and finally you said yes,

but in that way that always keeps me

longing for spins and dips, your hand

at my hip, my hair trembling to the floor.

Where You Touched My Arm

I have set up a bright,
yellow-and-white striped cabana to shade
the lively game of cards beneath,
all that shuffling and dealing,
the bids and passes, the hearts trumping
spades, the mints and chocolates,
the frosted glasses of pink lemonade served
on the hour and the curly-haired waiter
with the black tray
discreetly ducking under palms
to collect the empties and those
waves, those waves, how they kept insisting,
insisting until the whole shore shimmered.

Eve Begs Adam to Play His Guitar

She wants to watch him
belt out the words
to Guy Clark's "Fools for Each Other."
Or, if he'd rather, he can play
the CD and lip sync. It doesn't matter.
What matters is how she heats
when the music slinks
through her belly.

Who gave up when the fire burned low?
Who flew south when the wind blew cold?
Wasn't me, darling. Wasn't you.

Each stanza he sings melts
the old rage—the mornings he left her
waiting outside the laundromat,
holding a basket of wet sheets. The evenings
he lolled by the fire scratching
his groin, one infernal black jack
after another slapping the red queen.

We are fools for each other, me and you.
We are lovers, in fact, we've gone crazy out back,
like only fools for each other can do.

Adam croons

until her thighs fall loose

and she wants him

the way she wanted someone

to lift her, hot and bawling,

from the crib by the window,

lift her high out of the swelter of herself,

big hands on her back, way back

when she ground out of his side

like a baby—

had she ever been a baby

or even a child.

A Man Calls to Say My Son Is on a Farm for Alcoholics outside Jackson, Mississippi

We're famous all over
the state, he says. Eight weeks.
Christ-based. Not gonna find
many like us, ma'am. No smoking.
Hard labor sunup to sundown.
Grow our own food. Goats, pigs.
He like animals? Bible study.
Chapel every day. Twice
on Sunday. Clean, warm bed.
Most folk come in here
don't know much about the Bible.
Son's gonna be fine, if he stick with it,
do his part. Some leave, not many.
We're 'bout nine miles north of Jackson,
toward Yazoo City. Anybody want a drink,
gotta want a drink mighty bad
to walk down that blacktop
middle of the night or under the broil
of a noonday sun. Gotta be mighty
thirsty, gotta be dying for a drink,
ma'am. Gotta be flat-out dying.

The Other Life

The one by the ocean,

upstairs room with a view,

second row, an outside wooden stair . . .

I could have chosen that one,

climbing each night after work,

as a waitress maybe or clerk,

gauzy skirt whispering

at my ankle. Inside, one lamp

left burning, I settle cross-legged

on the bed, emptying quarters

into silvery pools, rolling them

into rounds of fives for the rent,

tens for the train trip to Arizona

next winter. Before supper,

filling the tub as the curtain drifts out

over the TV, revealing stars,

scattering last night's ashes.

Instead, I live inland

in the yellow house on the corner

across from the park. That's where

I am now, in the white chair

by the upstairs window,

pin oaks splashing the panes.

Don't misunderstand. I'm here by consent.
I was simply trying to remember
the exact dimensions of longing.

Eve's Out at the Edge

of evening again,
swinging on a banyan root,
wanting but not sure
what. Serpent, lounging
in the ferns, same old line:
Why not? Why not?

Eve singsongs: *God said
Adam and I will die
if we eat off that tree.*

Snake shrugs
a dusky shrug. She fiddles
with her hair. And where's
Adam? The man
who never seems to want
but has no trouble taking.

This time, serpent says,
*Nah. Y'all won't die. Eat
and your eyes'll fly open.*
Eve sidles to the tree,
cups the apple

before she bites, rubs it
against her cheek, tries
to fathom what she doesn't
know. Passion, yes. Joy.
Satisfaction, though that's low
on her scale. Right now,
her heart's as smooth
as French-milled soap. Not
for long. The day could come

when there's a son,
maybe two. Say one splinters
her heart when he leaves
his brother to bleed
in a stubborn field.
What then?
How will she feel
standing in the door
as he disappears
along the road, forever
marked? Or, day after day,
stacking and restackng
the plates, setting out bowls
before those vacant chairs.

The Wrong Dress

There you are

in a small, disjointed crowd,

wearing your old brown wool,

trying to claim someone's attention.

Be specific. You know exactly

who it is: the man

from the past who's smiling,

yes, though his eyes begin

to fasten on the blue

spine of distance. And you?

Do you ever ask why

you're never prepared

for the glistening chance

reeled in from the deep,

sleek and acrobatic,

the floor that dissolves

into a meadow for romance,

the wind that sings like a harp

in the pines, et cetera?

Someone whispers, *Wear*

close-fitting green, show off

your hips. No use. Right moment,

wrong dress. The ecstasy of regret.

Adam Tries to Explain to God
That None of This Is His Fault

She sliced it. Parted my lips,
pried my teeth, ground
that white meat into my mouth.
I could hardly breathe,
Eve at my cheek, panting:
Is it good? Is it good?

Exploding: *How dare you wander*
all those days among the trees
and not show one whit
of curiosity. How dare you!

As if I'd sinned against her.
As if I, not she, had disobeyed.

Relapse

I do not talk about this or want you to either.
It's about my son. I can't give you his name.
It is lodged in my throat, a dry leaf.

Did you ever read the book, *Mrs. Caldwell Speaks
to Her Son*? I opened it once to a story
about her dead child. I gnawed
like a rat along her words. "If you
had gotten lost in an abandoned garden,
Eliacim," she wrote, "in a murky garden
of willows and junipers, I would never tire
of looking for you, my dear, of looking
for you with lights and with the little hazelwood
wand which illuminates the waters
and hidden treasures. . . ."

Do these words stir you as they did me?
Mrs. Caldwell tells her son
that as a girl she herself lived near
such an abandoned garden. From morning
to night, she says to him,
mothers who had lost sons
walked and talked senselessly, their wands lit . . .

Back then, she says, she laughed, immune
to those miseries, as I, too, was immune
to certain miseries of my own childhood
behind the plumbago hedge,
behind the sea-grape tree, whose coarse,
fan-shaped leaves we often sprayed with gold.

Did I mention my son is alive?
What need, then, have I to wander
through murky gardens,
a hazelwood wand in hand?
I'll tell you my need: When I look at him,
I see through his presence into his absence.
I touch his shoulders and my fingers
encounter holes. It's been this way for years.
One drink, and he'll blow
right out of this world as you're drying
the tablespoons. One drink
and all I know of him evaporates.

When he called last night, his "hello"
broke like a yolk into the phone. Gone
again. So back I go, into the murky garden,
my wand shining dimly.
Where, where is my son?
If I crawl along the edge of the pond,
will I find him among the tadpoles and lilies?
Will I find him among the worms?

I must tell you, since reading *Mrs. Caldwell,*

I have razed my house, cleared the lot.

I now grow a healthy stand of trees,

though as you may know, the hazel

is not native to the Carolinas.

When weather permits, I set up

a table at the edge of the lane

and carve my wands. People stop to watch.

Some are only curious and soon wander away.

Others feel the need to touch and rub.

They'll try two or three, and when a wand fits

the hand, it is a marriage of absence

and presence. They nod. I reach

into my basket for a new branch to burn.

Leaving the Garden

Eve made the bed, squared
the corners. Touched
the walls. She wanted to grab
the needlepoint pillow
she finished last spring,
but they had to leave
everything. Violets
in bloom. Baby lambs.
The best broom
she'd ever have, brisk
and light. Adam emptied
the ashes into the roses,
propped his hoe. They rushed
out front to see
if the tulips were up,
ran back inside to set
the kitchen straight.
They spent time
they didn't have, threw out
bacon, cheese,
parsley gone limp
and black. The hateful figs
in clotted cream.

Suffused in the Heat

Scattered Typing

1.

Years ago,
in that upstairs room
with the black-lacquered
Chinese chest, your sister
in the arm chair,
legs folded under
her full dress, pregnant,
barely showing. You
turning my shoulders
toward the window,
slice of bay, red
and white sail. I still feel
your hands, your heat. Even today
I see that open sky,
the blue beyond
the blue. What's lost
tacks through me.

2.

I believe it lies
west of here, longing

without shape. I rise
before light, the trees singing
me onward. I will know it
by the low places
along the roads—
if there are roads—
the smell of shade
collecting under houses—
if there are houses.
Day after day, I drive
through forests, deserts,
along creeks. Still it lies west,
fierce and blue, untrekked.

3.

I pray for rain,
its cool burn,
pearly drift.
I'll watch it spatter
the wheelbarrow
and fill the blue jars
I use to outline
the flower beds.
The rain will silken
the rough strands
of my hair, thread

soft as milk
along my neck.
When you return,
I will gleam
from so much rain.
You'll touch me
and your fingers will shine.

4.

I drive miles
for the best view,
glide the arc
of a country bridge,
park, settle myself
on a hill, arms locked
around my knees.
Perfect vantage. Below,
the wedding party gathers
at the stone house
in the meadow.
The bride hesitates
at the door, shines through,
translucent, acres
of tulle. She looks up
to the bridge, waves.
We are radiant.

5.

Silk fan

of a November dawn

teases the pond

and the geese

as they rise

like scattered typing

from me toward

your frank brown house,

your wife at the stove

ready to weep or weeping.

6.

Once I baked a tart,

it stunned everyone

at the table, the pastry light,

the ingredients—goat cheese,

plum tomatoes, basil

from my garden—perfection.

When your letter arrived today,

I remembered that tart,

its secret, teasing steam,

how I carved it into wedges

while someone poured wine,

how we leaned back,

napkins drifting to our laps,

how we breathed deep,

suffused in the heat

that precedes a glad devouring.

7.

I pull stones from streams

and spread them in the sun

to study their warmth

at midday, full and hot

like good bread

you eat on a blanket

with someone you love, cooling

by late afternoon

to the tiles

in that smoky hotel bar

with the palms and the parrots

where we waited and waited for a table,

waited for drinks, for music, for change,

for luck, waited for words

I'm still digging up.

Eve's Growing Concern

Whose the greater crime?
He ate. He ate.
Never doubted what I gave.
Never asked why.

I watched him try
to clean the blade.
Whose the greater crime?
He ate. He ate.

I watched the juice slide
down his face,
watched him grimace
and shield his eyes.
Whose the greater crime?
He ate. He ate.

After Detox

He could drink the river.
He could drink the river dry.
He's sitting on the bank,
clasping his knees, vines trembling
around him. Each time he looks across
the water, he imagines the field,
the field with cows and a few crows,
and beyond the pasture
with its oval pond, bare oaks
about a cabin. Always the same path,
the one crooked window, the door
flimsy as a ghost. This is the picture
he drew as a child, repeatedly.
This is what he believes
he will find on the other side.

All I can do is watch
from my kitchen, crack
these eggs, open the jar of jelly.
He'll smell the bacon and climb
toward home. Here comes my son
who is made of cravings. Here comes

my son who is made of gauze. I hold
open the door, my arms stiff as pine.
Here comes my son, my son.

Deprivation

The ultimate grief:
to know you've grown fat
on it, sucked the marrow,
sopped the plate,
and that even later,
when the curtain falls,
when the band packs up,
when the saxophone player
stashes his comb
in his back pocket
and heads for the telephones,
you can't refuse the waiters
passing eclairs, always grateful
for that final morsel
that makes you feel so full
you can walk away starving.

Eve's Sorrows Multiplying

For weeks she's sick
at her stomach.
Only mint leaves ease
the waves that heave
behind her tongue.
Will she be one again,
rid of the kicking
that threatens
to split her?
Will she love it
the way Adam loves her
papaya breasts?

The baby balls his fists, rages,
as if the dreadful air
might finish him. She tells Adam
to bundle them in skins.

This is a new thing, she thinks. *Like us
but not us. If I fail
to comprehend him, who will?*

Dread Begs to Fondle Your Breasts

Dread, bent, hobbles up the back steps,
begging to fondle your breasts.
Pinch-penny lips, gnarled stick rapping,
he lacks both charm and manners.

He's begging to fondle your breasts
and requests a clean, downy cot.
He lacks both charm and manners
as he strokes your arm, elbow to wrist.

He requests a clean, downy cot
so he can settle his knobby bones.
As he strokes your arm, elbow to wrist,
your heart's a sawmill spewing fear.

So he can settle his knobby bones,
you offer your crispest linens.
Your heart's a sawmill spewing fear,
dry flecks fly in your face and sting.

You offer your crispest linens.
His finger on your nipple's rough.
Dry flecks fly in your face and sting.
Still, you hang his coat in the hall.

His finger on your nipple's rough,
too rough to stir your passion.
Still, you hang his coat in the hall,
elbows worn, dandruff on the cuffs.

Too rough to stir your passion,
he cups a breast in each thin hand,
elbows worn, dandruff on the cuffs.
Dread is making himself at home.

He cups a breast in each thin hand,
sucking hungry like a baby.
Dread is making himself at home,
and you won't dare to charge him rent.

Sucking hungry like a baby,
pinch-penny lips, gnarled stick rapping,
and you won't dare to charge him rent.
Dread, bent, hobbles up the back steps.

Eve Dreams of Mary Todd Lincoln

Her husband's pillow, soaked with blood,
Mary's bending
to stroke and kiss
his shattered skull,

the generals dragging her out,
screaming, writhing
in their hot grip,
their smell of wet

wool. In that bed, her darling Abe,
eye bloated, blue–
black. She's reaching
to touch. Doctors

shout, *Get out!* Room's hushed
but for his rattle and
down the long hall,
those awful sobs.

I Hang Up the Phone after Hearing I Have Cancer

and remember that frigid March
I was six and convinced
my cousins, a year older,
we'd be allowed
at our grandmother's funeral
only if we wore our coats
backward. That way, I told them,
no one would know who we are.
We took turns buttoning
each other up, absorbed
in our new tedium.
As we walked, sun lit
the high branches, the air
was smart and clean.
At the church, a man stepped out.
He wore a hat, his palms were wide
and pink. He turned us around,
marched us home, our coats
still buttoned up the back.
The sun spread itself pale
on the porch steps. The door
rattled shut behind us.
We huddled in the dark
front hall, fingers stiff, buttons ice.

At a Flea Market, A Woman Buys a Letter Postmarked 1944, From Sybil Reed to Louis Mack

She buys it for the same reason
I might—to unearth her life, to try
to decipher its redeemable parts:
What she might've said,
whom she might've loved and how.

As she reads, a photo
of a hula dancer—grass skirt, lei,
and Sybil's bright scrawl "Taken
in Hawaiian Islands at a famous nite spot"—
falls from the envelope. I'm hoping
the woman will toss the letter,
its powdery sentiments, its tepid longings,
and keep the picture that slipped out
like a song or a charm, about an easy,
hibiscus-in-the-hair kind of love.

 No, I'm sad to say, she crumples
the photo, stuffs it deep
into her purse, heads to another booth
where she lifts an old glass pitcher
to the sun, running a slow finger
around the rim. Chip or flaw,
she will not succumb, no matter the luster.

I've done the same: doused
the impulse to sail
beyond the familiar harbor.
The woman's lost to me now,
and soon I won't even recall
the tune she hummed
when she handed over her quarter.

The Wink

He sees me heading
into the Detox lobby
with Marlboros and quarters,
and he darts in from the patio,
wearing green, hospital-issue pajamas
and paper slippers. We hug, he nods
his thanks, says, *I'm gonna be all right.*

And he gives me this sly wink.

My own son.

A wino's wink.
A wink that reeks.
I want to scream:

Don't you dare, boy!

I'm staring at the creases
the wink left in his cheek, wanting
to sand his face smooth
and—wait—in a flash I know
the wink could unlatch my gold

anklet, snatch my freshwater pearls,

wheedle me out of everything

I own, including my life

savings, dash out the door,

everything gone in a wink.

To the Neighbor Whose Gardenias I Stole Last Spring

I'm leaving these miniature cakes
on your doorstep
as recompense.
Did you happen

to see me rip blooms from your hedge?
I could not help
myself. Sorrow
had wedged its way

into my heart, the delicate scent
of your flowers
cradling me in
balm. Enjoy these

cakes. I've laced them with rum. Come next
spring I can't say
for certain I
won't steal again.

The Vaster Blue

She Never Thought of Vegetables

Never imagined
she'd turn her back
on flowers, until furrows,
brown and silent, creased
her sleep. She could feel her soul
fold cool and green, compose itself,
furling, holding its shape,
unlike those humid fellowships
of petals, inhaling, exhaling,
their breakneck dreaming,
their relentless basking,
scent their only return
and scant.

The Day Before My Father Died

I swear to you I saw them—
a row of tombstones,
granite, engraved:
Asleep In His Bosom,
Angels Tend Him Now,
where moments before
had been nothing
but shore, a few
bleached shells,
water so clear
I saw a school
of yellow fish
dart in filtered sun.
I wanted to grab one,
feel it spasm
against my palm.
But it was quick
and flashed away.

Wake the Tree

the tree inside you. Climb
to the top and see
the tall buildings.
They are swaying
in the breeze.
They catch the sun
and gleam. A fleece
of green covers you,
and your arms make a V
as if you're lifting
a branch to the sky.

Your father stands
below with his camera.
He wants to catch you
before you fall
into your mother,
into your woman flesh.
Today, you are made
of sticks, lust a leaf pile
behind the wall.
He likes you
this way, before

it all happens,
before the fattening
and the blood. Hold
still, he says. The grass
is asleep. The sky
enameled with girl.

Better to Know the Woodcutter Might Never Arrive At the Cottage

My son calls again drunk,
this time from Lafayette, Louisiana,

where he says not to worry,
he's with a woman named Peg,

and at last it sinks in
that I prefer reality's dry smack

to hope's butterfly kisses.
Better to know

the flannel-shirted woodcutter
might never arrive in time

to slice the old woman free
of the wolf's slick belly,

her papery fist blue
from pounding the hot stall

of his ribs, her thin ear raw
from straining to hear

the saving rap-rap at the door.

How well I know

that suffocating trap,

know I may never step forward

into light, blinking once

or twice before I accept

the basket of wildflowers and brie,

before I gather to my breast

the smiling, familiar child.

The Reconstructed Breast

She's now the dumb sister,
the sister who can't
even hum. Once she knew
everything: the blister of winter
before it arrived, the ocean's
swelter and churn. The smart sister
can remember when they thrilled
to the words of "Earth Angel,"
swam naked to the sand bar,
dozed in the suck and slap
of Biscayne Bay.

To vex the dumb sister,
the smart one's taken to trilling
names of old loves. *David,*
she sings. *Warren. Ed.*
The dumb one
blinks once or twice,
mute or stunned.
In bed, she rolls over
close: *Do you love me still?*
Before the smart one
can answer, the dumb sister's already
plumped her pillows and is drowsing.

Eve's Not a Bad Mimic

and she's got God down
pat. *Oh, Adam, where are you?*
Around every corner, down
every alley: *Where are you, Adam?*

She nags him
until he blanches,
and that little palpitation
on his nostril
when she catches him
at some mischief
is, to her, delicious.

You're probably thinking
Adam's a saint, long-suffering,
patient, devoted. Eve,
you say, is wicked, mean,
forever bedeviling.

Listen. Next time you hear her
badgering Adam, remember
that inlet where she slept,
a mere ribbon inside

his chest. Feel the tornado
sucking her out, air slapping
at her flesh. She's dripping wet,
knees wobbly. And Adam?
Slathered in sleep.

In the Two-Week Relapse Prevention Program My Son Writes a Forty-Six-Page Autobiography

1. Back Steps

Brother gone off
to a fair with the neighborhood kids
and by the time the shadow
of that pine touches these steps,
I know, know in my belly,
they'll remember they forgot
me. Turn around. Come back.
Any minute. Just wait.

2. The Accident

To this day, nobody ever says Leg
or Arm or Smashed Bike or Speeding Car
or Front Teeth Knocked Out. It's always
the Accident. April. Sunday. Pavement.
Dad, hands in pockets, leaning over. His gold
necklace. Frozen mom. A stranger's arms.
Ambulance. Mom climbing in. *Somebody,
please put away the groceries.*

Body cast sawed in two. Dust floating
in tight square cubicle. Hot smell. *Try to keep him*

out of trees, at least for the next few weeks.
Laughter flattening against cream walls.

3. Divorce

Nobody called it Divorce. They called it
the Lake. They said Before the Lake. After
the Lake, as if a huge curl of water
had scooped us up and washed us away.

4. Kissing

Mom's in Dad's lap on the screened porch
in the darker-than-lake dark, rocking. Creep
to the sliding glass door. Don't breathe.
She's talking about hurricanes. What cuts
across the grain. Her hands in the air.
Slice. Slice. *What if we'd waited a year to marry?*
she asks. *Impossible,* he says. *Would've battered
my ego.* They're kissing. *Do you hear
me? I said, kissing.* Divorce or no divorce.

5. Yellow Bowls

Third grade starts. Brick apartment
in town. Fifth floor. Brother's shoes
on the stone balcony, stink curdling
the air. Dad at the lake. Mom, on tiptoe,
stacking yellow bowls on the shelves. Clink.

Clink. Humming. The whole kitchen's
a yellow bowl. Windows open. Blue breeze.

Leave them in the box, I say. *Leave the bowls
in the box.* Susan at the door. Red hair.
Red lips. Green plant in a basket. They can't open
the wine. Susan drives a nail in the cork. Light
like sand dollars on the ceiling. They're laughing.
Ancient elevator. Stick out your hand. Snatch it
back before the brass gate slams. Stick it out.
Snatch it back. *Be careful, please!* she calls
down the shaft. Going down.
Scare her. Get smashed. Get smashed.

The Woman Who Only Went up to the Neck

She could still entertain
thoughts, although she didn't know

how. People recognized her.
She didn't understand

why. Once a man told her he knew her
by her hair, and she wondered

what held it on.
Why didn't it blow off

when she stepped down from a bus
or pushed through a revolving door?

She could see, too. In fact,
she could see her own hair. It was dark

red and lay in close, sculpted waves.
But close to what? The hair

bore no resemblance to the hair
she used to grow. You must be wondering

how she lost her head. If there was an occasion,
a passion so great metaphor became fact.

I have no idea. I can tell you only this: One day,
as she was walking out to pay her light bill,

she caught sight of her head resting
on a bench, waiting, she guessed, on a ride

or a friend. Stranger still, she noticed
the head was blushing. The woman didn't speak

or even nod but reached out with her bare hand
to stroke the hair, her own crimson kin.

Never Mind My Own Sweet Cottage

I am so thin
my rings drop off
my fingers and roll across
the floor, the old hunger gone.
For years, I knelt in the yard
fingering the chicken bone
the boy poked through
the slats. Was I tricked? Yes,
yes. No need to deny it.
For months I plotted
how to fatten those kids,
serving up my best kuchen
and strudel. All those trips
to the pen, back and forth, back
and forth, sun scorching my neck,
flies speckling my apron. Never mind
my own sweet cottage, undusted, .
unswept. I wanted nothing
that was mine. Even the orphans' crumbs
winked at me like diamonds.

A Reason to Embrace Sorrow

The creek stitches
through the park
a mystery its beginning
where wet first sought wet.

From this bridge
we drop our string
of sorrows down
into the drift
where they become loose
and buoyant, sailing
past leaves that trap
their float toward the vaster blue.

We didn't imagine
they could navigate
with such ease
never dreamed
they'd fall in love
with each other
rent an apartment
with a view, grow
geraniums on the balcony

throw buckets of suds
across the tile floor
get down on their knees
to scrub before finding
the lace cloth
and lighting candles.

Call it lack of imagination.

We stroll home bereft
our backs to the moon.

What Happened to My Parents

In late-middle age,
they built a white house
with a wood-burning stove.
My father planted tomatoes
and beans. My mother
set out ferns.
My sons helped
to build a low rock wall
along the drive.

Evenings, the fire popped
and cracked. One day,
my father cut down
a swaying sweetgum
to make more room
for his garden,
and he tape-recorded
the raucous stutter of the saw.

Before you knew it,
they'd both died,
one after another, my father
on an April morning

during his bath.
My mother, that July,
a pot of beans burning
on the stove.

I play the tape
from time to time,
straining to hear
what they were saying
to each other
as the old tree crashed.
No matter how high
I turn the volume,
their words keep flying off,
scattering into that blast
of sudden blue.

The Chair Where I Sat Reading While My Parents Made Love

was not a big chair.
I could haul it all over
the house. Usually
I dragged it to the back
screened porch where I sat
trying to make sense
of words, sounding them out,
their wildness crowding
my mouth as I practiced
each knobby line
again and again
until I had it down smooth
as a kiss, rocking
all the while, licking
my lips as if I were grown.
Page after page
like this until at last
I was lifted, lifted
out of my small chair.

I Try to Tear Myself Away from a Jigsaw Puzzle during the Last Minutes of Vacation

I can't resist one last fit,

maybe two, the tapered bentwood leg

or the edge of the violin case

open on the yellow chair. Such bliss

to find the piece that makes the room

come true. But what's the use?

In minutes we'll be gone, the puzzle

rattling home with us, breaking apart,

Matisse's red footstool and skirted table

tumbling down to his blue, blue sea.

A week before he died, morphine pack

at his waist, my father leaned against

his maple tree, explaining

to my husband in robust detail

how he'd like his gutters cleaned. The job

was not complete, he insisted,

until we'd plunged the garden hose

deep into the down-spouts, flushing out

all traces of debris. How he carried on,

as if he'd live for weeks. Back inside,

we unlaced his shoes, laid him down to nap.

I sift the pieces one more time, searching
for the elusive crease in the white
pleated curtains. I hear my husband turning off
the shower, and I must stop now,
gather sandals, camera, keys. Wait. This vague hint
of green might finish off the table skirt.

He's behind me now, smelling of soap
and aftershave. *Time,* he whispers at my neck,
to put away the puzzle. Together, we fold
the picture into the box: the chair
and footstool, the figures on the beach,
and between the balusters, the frail legs
of sunlight basking one more moment
on the diamond-patterned rug.

Long Distance

—for ECG

Folding clothes folding
you into the crook

the hardened thief
of my shoulder

I steal up the stairs
with the laundry

with your voice
your voice I haven't heard

in thirty years
I drove straight through

basement to bedroom
kitchen and back

your words a sack
of coins I stash

on every floor
They told me you married

the week before
knocked my legs

right out from under me
deep in the cedar chest

God forbid anything
should happen

to either of our spouses
into a crevice

in the attic studio
be there this time

wait for me
into the dish towels

the ordinary blue
and white striped

cotton dish towels
I will use to shine

every cup every
spoon in the house

Sometimes They Just Lie There

the light catching this bone
or that. Their vast sheen
could put out God's eye.
No old lover she's pining
for. No other nipple
hardens in his mind. Adam
can only measure Eve
by Eve, and Eve holds no one
up to Adam. They could sail
to Byzantium on this
kind of ease, bellies rising
and sinking, the old blood-soaked field
long dried. Let them sleep.
Before dawn, Eve might well slam out
the back door. Last night,
she mentioned a bird she'd seen,
how it lifted off the fence,
its white wings taking on a tinge
of green, a green so rich
she said her nostrils burned.